PARTS OF A PLANT

A Look at Flowers

Lindsey Lowe

KidHaven
PUBLISHING

Published in 2020 by
KidHaven Publishing, an Imprint of
Greenhaven Publishing, LLC
353 3rd Avenue
Suite 255
New York, NY 10010

For Brown Bear Books Ltd:
Text and Editor: Lindsey Lowe
Children's Publisher: Anne O'Daly
Design Manager: Keith Davis
Picture Manager: Sophie Mortimer

Picture Credits
t=top, c=center, b=bottom, l=left, r=right
Interior: Alamy: Zuma Press Inc 7; Dreamstime: Iryna Kolesova 21, Ondrej Prosicky 11t, Nokolay Stolmenov 19t; iStock: 8, 18b, 20, Debi Bishop 11b, Jiri Hrebicek 14-15, Elrond Peredhil 12b; Shutterstock: 9t, 10, 17br, 18, 501room 5b, Peter Fuzia 12-13, David havel 15b, Kaye Menner Photography 14b, Cathy Keifer 13b, My Sunnyday 6, Is Petia 19b, Quang ho 16, 17bc, Manfred Ruckszio 4, stocker1970 16-17, J Walter Terry Jr 5t, Laura VN 16b Duan Yongkang 9b.
All other photos and artwork, Brown Bear Books.

Cataloging-in-Publication Data

Names: Lowe, Lindsey.
Title: A look at flowers / Lindsey Lowe.
Description: New York : KidHaven Publishing, 2020. | Series: Parts of a plant | Includes glossary and index.
Identifiers: ISBN 9781534533615 (pbk.) | ISBN 9781534533639 (library bound) | ISBN 9781534533622 (6 pack) | ISBN 9781534533646 (ebook)
Subjects: LCSH: Flowers--Juvenile literature. | Flowers--Physiology--Juvenile literature. | Plant anatomy--Juvenile literature.
Classification: LCC QK49.L694 2020 | DDC 582.13--dc23

Manufactured in the United States of America

CPSIA Compliance Information: Batch #BW20KL:
For further information contact Greenhaven Publishing LLC, New York, New York at 1-844-317-7404.

Contents

What Are Flowers?

Flowers are not just for show. They make the fruits and seeds that will grow into new plants.

Plants that make flowers are called flowering plants. Some flowers are easy to see. Roses, tulips, pansies, petunias, and sunflowers have big, colorful flowers. Other plants have flowers that are harder to spot. Grasses have tiny green or white flowers. Most trees are flowering plants, too.

Wildflower meadows are important feeding and nesting sites for all kinds of insects, birds, and small animals.

THAT'S AMAZING!

Some plants have flowers that open for a very short time. The titan arum plant from Indonesia has giant red flowers that are 10 feet (3 m) tall. They appear for only a few days every 20 years!

Cherry Blossom

In Japan, the first cherry blossom marks the end of winter. Trees mostly blossom in early April. The flowers only last for four to seven days. In Japan, people celebrate Hanami, when cherry trees are covered in pink blossoms. People have picnics under the trees.

Inside a Flower

Flowers come in many shapes, sizes, and colors. Every part of a flower has an important job to do.

Most flowers have male parts called stamens. They make the pollen. Flowers also have a female part called a pistil. This makes eggs. Pollen sticks to the stigma. It travels down the style and fertilizes the eggs. Seeds grow inside the ovary.

Some flowers can pollinate themselves. Their anthers brush pollen straight onto their stigma. This is called self-pollination. Most flowers need to get pollen from another plant. This is called cross-pollination. Petals attract insects and birds, which carry pollen from the anther of one flower to the stigma of another.

Parts of a Flower

1 Petals attract insects and birds.

2 Stamens make the flower pollen.

3 Anthers at the top of the stamens hold the pollen.

4 Stigma at the top of the pistil receives pollen from another flower.

5 Pistil has three parts: stigma, style, and ovary.

6 Ovary grows new plant seeds from its fertilized eggs.

THAT'S AMAZING!

Some plants, like grasses, are pollinated by the wind. Pollen grains are tiny. They look like dust. When the wind blows, grasses produce clouds of pollen (see left) to make sure that at least one grain lands on another grass flower!

All Kinds of Flowers

All flowering plants do the same job. But their flowers can look very different.

Some flowers have three petals. Others have four or five. Harebells have flowers that are shaped like a cup. Petunia and bluebell flowers are bell-shaped.

Winter Bloomer

Most flowers bloom in the spring and summer, when it is warm. But a few plants, such as the yellow winter aconite, can survive on cold mountaintops. It blooms in January and February, even when snow is on the ground.

Forests

Many forest flowers bloom in spring, before the trees have grown all their leaves. The warm sunlight can reach the flowers. Bluebells flower from April to June. It can take seven years for a bluebell to flower.

THAT'S AMAZING!

Cacti live in hot deserts where it might not rain for years. Cactus flowers only bloom after it has rained. Even then, the hot desert sun quickly burns the soft petals. The flowers of the night-blooming cereus cactus (right) only open at night when it is cool. The flower dies the next day!

Flowers and Bees

Bees collect pollen from flowers. They use it as food. They also carry it to other flowers.

Most flowers use animals to spread their pollen. The most important pollinators are bees, butterflies, moths, and birds. Flowers have bright petals and sweet smells that attract bees. The flowers make a sugary water called nectar. The bees visit flowers to sip the nectar and gather pollen. They take the nectar back to the hive to make honey.

When a bee sips nectar from a flower, it brushes against the anthers. Pollen from the anthers sticks to the bee.

THAT'S AMAZING!

Most flowers attract bees with color and smell. The bee orchid has a different method. The flower looks like a female bee! Male bees visit the flower and try to mate with it. The orchid's pollen sticks to the bee's furry body. When the bee visits another plant, it takes the pollen to the flower.

Pollen Baskets

When a bee visits a flower it sips the nectar with its long tongue. It collects pollen in sacks on its legs called pollen baskets. As it pushes into the flower, it gets more pollen on its body. Some of this brushes off onto the other flowers the bee visits.

Butterflies and Moths

Butterflies and moths visit flowers to drink their nectar. They spread pollen and help pollinate the flowers.

Butterflies and moths sip nectar with their long tongues. Butterflies visit flowers that are open during the day. Most moths fly at night. They visit flowers that open at night, such as jasmine and evening primrose.

Perfect Partners

Yucca plants and yucca moths need each other to survive. The moth's caterpillars only eat yucca plant seeds. The yucca plant can only be pollinated by the yucca moth.

Hawkmoths

Hawkmoths have long tongues. They can reach inside narrow flowers. The moth sucks up the nectar and picks up pollen on its legs and wings. It carries the pollen to other flowers.

THAT'S AMAZING!

Milkweed leaves are poisonous to most insects. But monarch caterpillars eat them without being harmed. The poison from the leaves makes the caterpillars poisonous to birds. The birds don't eat the caterpillars, which grow and change into butterflies!

Flowers and Birds

In some parts of the world, many flowers are pollinated by birds. The pollen sticks to the bird's beak.

Flowers that rely on birds make a lot of nectar. But they have to make sure that only the right birds get it. The flowers are often shaped like long tubes. Only birds with long, thin beaks can reach the nectar.

Seeing Red

Birds have a poor sense of smell, but they see colors clearly. Flowers that attract birds are often bright red. The red flowering gum tree attracts the Australian rainbow lorikeet to feed on its nectar.

Hummingbirds

Hummingbirds have long, thin beaks. The birds hover in the air while they feed on the flower nectar. This uses a lot of energy. Hummingbirds need to eat half their body weight in nectar every day.

THAT'S AMAZING!

Most flowers are pollinated by insects and birds. But some are pollinated by mice and rats. In Australia, some flowers are even pollinated by frogs! Others, like the flowers of the saguaro cactus, are pollinated by bats (right). All these animals are attracted by the sweet nectar.

Flowers for Gardens

In the past, flowers only grew wild. But people liked them so much they began to grow them in gardens.

Over hundreds of years, gardeners changed wild plants. They planted seeds of flowers with large petals or bright colors. Sometimes they mixed pollen from different flowers. A red flower mixed with a blue flower gave a purple flower. Over time, some flowers would only grow in gardens.

Garden Favorites

Here are some popular garden flowers. How many have you seen? Do you have any of them in your backyard or window box?

Petunia

Dahlia

THAT'S AMAZING!

In the Netherlands, tulips are grown on huge flower farms. Tulips were taken to Holland from Turkey in the 1500s. They were very expensive to buy. Some people became rich selling them. This period was called "Tulipomania." In 1637, a single tulip bulb cost the price of a house! As a result, people stopped buying them. The price dropped. Tulips became flowers that most people could afford to buy.

About three billion tulips are grown in the Netherlands every year!

Daisy

Black-Eyed Susan

Rose

Peony

Flowers for Scent

Flowers make scents to attract pollinators. People use the scents to make perfume.

A flower's scent comes from oils in the petals. These are called essential oils. Usually, the less color a petal has, the more oil it makes. This makes the scent stronger. White flowers are the strongest smelling, followed by pale yellow and pale pink. Flowers most often used for perfumes are roses, violets, jasmine, lavender, and lilies. The smell of lavender can also help people sleep.

Lavender flowers smell sweet. The oil is used in soaps, bath crystals, and perfumes.

THAT'S AMAZING!

Rose Valley in Bulgaria is famous for roses. Millions of pink Damask roses are picked here from May to June each year. The flowers are picked by hand early in the morning. They are collected in large willow baskets. It takes 60,000 rose petals to make just 1 ounce (30 g) of oil!

Eating Flowers

Flowers smell nice. Some flowers also taste nice. Saffron is a spice used to flavor food. It comes from the dried stigma and style of a crocus called the saffron crocus. The petals are purple, but the stigma and style are bright orange.

Grow It!

Sunflower seeds are easy to grow in pots from mid-April to May. Ask an adult to buy a packet of garden sunflower seeds and some soil-based potting compost.

Here's How

- Fill some plastic cups with potting compost. Water the compost to make it damp.
- Make a small hole in the middle of the compost with your finger. Do the same in each cup.
- Drop a single sunflower seed into each hole, cover with a layer of compost, and spray with water.
- Put the cups on a sunny windowsill. Check them every day. Spray them with water if the compost feels dry.
- Shoots will appear after 5 to 10 days. When your plants have grown too big for the plastic cups, transfer each plant to a bigger flowerpot. Water regularly. You might have to support the stems with a stick tied loosely to the stalk if the plant grows very tall.
- Your sunflowers should flower after about 8 weeks. When the sunflower heads turn brown, cut them off and put them somewhere to dry completely. Gently rub off the seeds and put them outside for the birds to eat.

Cook It!

WARNING
Most cooking involves chopping ingredients and heating them in some way. Be careful as you cook and make sure an adult kitchen assistant is around to help!

Lavender tastes great in a lemon drizzle cake!

2 ½ cups plain flour
2 tsp baking powder
2 sticks soft butter
1 cup caster sugar
1 tbsp edible lavender (available at supermarkets)
zest of 2 large lemons
3 large eggs, beaten
¾ cup milk

For the drizzle:

juice of 2 large lemons
½ cup caster sugar

Here's How

1. Preheat the oven to 350°F (180°C). Line a loaf pan with greaseproof paper.
2. Put the flour, baking powder, butter, sugar, lavender, lemon zest (save the juice), and beaten eggs in a food processor.
3. Mix on low speed until the ingredients combine. Add the milk gradually, then mix on high speed until the batter is smooth. Pour the batter into the loaf pan.
4. Bake for about 55 minutes, or until a skewer inserted in the center comes out clean. Remove from the oven but leave the cake in the pan.
5. Prick holes in the cake with a skewer. Sprinkle with more lavender. Mix the lemon juice and sugar together. Spoon it over the cake and leave to cool completely in the pan before removing it.

Glossary

anther The pollen-coated tip of a flower's stamen.

blooms The colorful flowers of a plant, usually with petals.

blossom The flower of a tree and other plants.

caterpillar A butterfly in the first stage of its life, with a wormlike body.

essential oil A scent oil made in a flower's petals.

fertilize When pollen reaches the plant's ovary and joins with the egg to make a seed.

flowering plant Any plant that has flowers.

nectar The sugary liquid made by flowers.

pistil A flower's female part, where eggs are made into seeds.

pollen The powder made by a flower's male parts.

pollination The joining of pollen to a flower's female parts.

pollinators Animals, such as bees and butterflies, that pollinate flowers.

stamen One of a flower's male parts, where the pollen is made.

Further Resources

Books

Amstutz, Lisa J. *Investigating Plant Life Cycles.* Minneapolis MN: Lerner Publishing, 2016.

Bodach, Vijaya Khisty. *Flowers* (Plant Parts). Mankato, MN: Capstone Press, 2016.

Dickmann, Nancy. *Q & A About Plants* (Curious Nature). New York: Powerkids Press, 2017.

Messner, Kate. *Up in the Garden and Down in the Dirt*. San Francisco: Chronicle Books, 2017.

Websites

https://www.scienceforkidsclub.com/flowering-plants.html

https://kids.kiddle.co/Flower

Publisher's note to educators and parents: Our editors have carefully reviewed these websites to ensure that they are suitable for students. Many websites change frequently, however, and we cannot guarantee that a site's future contents will continue to meet our high standards of quality and educational value. Be advised that students should be closely supervised whenever they access the Internet.

Index